the
Sacred
Harvest

WELCOME

LEECH LAKE
INDIAN RESERVATION

NO SPECIAL LICENSE REQUIRED EXCEPT
FOR COMMERCIAL TAKING OF WILD RICE,
MINNOWS, AND OTHER BAIT.

UP TO $500 FINE FOR DAMAGING OR REMOVING THIS SIGN

WE ARE STILL HERE

NATIVE AMERICANS TODAY

the Sacred Harvest

Ojibway Wild Rice Gathering

Gordon Regguinti

Photographs by Dale Kakkak

With a Foreword by Michael Dorris

 Lerner Publications Company

Series Editor: Gordon Regguinti
Series Consultants: W. Roger Buffalohead, Juanita G. Corbine Espinosa

Illustrations by Carly Bordeau. The floral illustrations are based on Ojibway beadwork designs.

This book is available in two editions:
Library binding by Lerner Publications Company, a division of Lerner Publishing Group
Soft cover by First Avenue Editions, an imprint of Lerner Publishing Group
241 First Avenue North
Minneapolis, MN 55401 U.S.A.

Website address: www.lernerbooks.com

Library of Congress Cataloging-in-Publication Data

Regguinti, Gordon.
   The sacred harvest : Ojibway wild rice gathering / by Gordon
Regguinti : photographs by Dale Kakkak: foreword by Michael Dorris.
      p. cm. — (We are still here)
   Includes bibliographical references (p. 47).
   Summary: Glen Jackson, Jr., an eleven-year-old Ojibway Indian in
northern Minnesota, goes with his father to harvest wild rice, the
sacred food of his people.
   ISBN 0-8225-2650-6 (lib. bdg. : alk. paper)
   ISBN 0-8225-9620-2 (pbk. : alk. paper)
   1. Ojibwa Indians—Food—Juvenile literature. 2. Ojibwa Indians—
Social life and customs—Juvenile literature. 3. Wild rice—
Minnesota—Leech Lake Indian Reservation—Harvesting—Juvenile
literature. 4. Leech Lake Indian Reservation (Minn.)—Social life
and customs—Juvenile literature. [1. Ojibwa Indians—Social life
and customs. 2. Indians of North America—Social life and customs.
3. Wild rice—Harvesting. 4. Jackson, Glen.] I. Kakkak, Dale,
ill. II. Title. III. Series.
E99.C6R297   1992
977.6'82—dc20   92-1167

Manufactured in the United States of America
3 4 5 6 7 8 – JR – 06 05 04 03 02 01

This book is dedicated to my children:
Michael, Shanah, Naush, Andrew, Grace, Joseph;
to my granddaughter, Briana;
and to the spirit of the child who has traveled on.
May the children of the world enjoy a life
full of the beauties of creation.

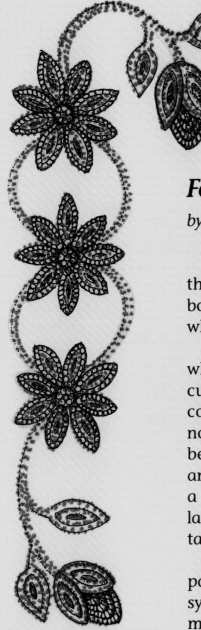

Foreword

by Michael Dorris

How do we get to be who we are? What are the ingredients that shape our values, customs, language, and tastes, that bond us into a unit different from any other? On a large scale, what makes the Swedes Swedish or the Japanese Japanese?

These questions become even more subtle and interesting when they're addressed to distinct and enduring traditional cultures coexisting within the boundaries of a large and complex society. Certainly Americans visiting abroad have no trouble recognizing their fellow countrymen and women, be they black or white, descended from Mexican or Polish ancestors, rich or poor. As a people, we have much in common, a great deal that we more or less share: a recent history, a language, a common denominator of popular music, entertainment, and politics.

But, if we are fortunate, we also belong to a small, more particular community, defined by ethnicity or kinship, belief system or geography. It is in this intimate circle that we are most "ourselves," where our jokes are best appreciated, our special dishes most enjoyed. These are the people to whom we go first when we need comfort or empathy, for they speak our own brand of cultural shorthand, and always know the correct things to say, the proper things to do.

The Sacred Harvest provides an insider's view into just such a world, that of the contemporary Ojibway people. If we are ourselves Ojibway, we will probably nod often while reading these pages, affirming the familiar, approving that this tribal family keeps alive and passes on the "right" way to collect and process *mahnomin*, or wild rice. If we belong to another tribe, we will follow this special journey of initiation and education with interest, gaining respect for a way of doing things that's rich and rewarding.

This is a book about people who are neither exotic nor unusual. If you encountered them at a shopping mall or at a movie theater they might seem at first glance like anyone else, a mother and father proud of their son, American as apple pie. *The Sacred Harvest* does not dispute this picture, but it does expand it. The Jackson family of Leech Lake Reservation are also as American as wild rice.

Michael Dorris is the author of *A Yellow Raft in Blue Water, The Broken Cord*, and, with Louise Erdrich, *The Crown of Columbus*. His first book for children is *Morning Girl*.

*F*or 11-year-old Glen Jackson, Jr., this warm, late summer day was important. It was a day he had waited for all year. It was the first time his father Glen Sr. would take him out to gather *mahnomin* (pronounced mah-NO-men), the sacred food of the Ojibway people. This was the day he would become a wild ricer.

As Glen and his father dragged the canoe down the narrow path toward the Bowstring River, Glen wondered if he would be strong enough to push the boat through the thick wild rice bed. Would he be able to keep it straight? Would he lose his balance and tip the canoe like other people he had heard stories about?

When they arrived at the river's edge, his father told Glen that they would take it easy—the day was meant for learning. They loaded their gear into the canoe, climbed in, and pushed off, gliding slowly across the shallow, murky water toward the wild rice.

Every summer since he could remember, Glen had wanted to gather wild rice. As the harvest approached each year, the people in his town were busy preparing their boats, knockers, and poles. In his own family, wild rice was the main topic of conversation during many meals. His parents talked about where the rice was growing best that season and planned which beds they would harvest. Several times Glen had waited at the boat landing for his parents to come back from the rice bed, eager to help them pull their boatload of rice onshore. Now he would be taking part in the harvest himself.

Glen is the only child of Glen and Darlene Jackson. They live in Inger, a town of about 200 people in northern Minnesota. Glen's grandmother, most of his uncles and aunts, and many of his cousins also live in Inger. The town straddles the Bowstring River near the eastern border of the Leech Lake Reservation.

Glen Sr., Glen Jr., and Darlene Jackson relax at home.

Much of the reservation is covered with huge forests of birch, pine, oak, and maple trees. Deer, bears, wolves, and other animals live in the woods. Walleye, muskellunge, whitefish, pike, and bass are plentiful in the many rivers and lakes within the borders of the 1,058-square-mile (2,740-square-kilometer) reservation.

Inger is a small town on the Leech Lake Reservation.

11

As Glen began his first day as a ricer, his father handed him the long wooden pole that he would use to push the boat through the dense stalks of wild rice growing in the wide river. His father sat just in front of Glen in the canoe, holding the knockers—the slender sticks used to knock the rice into the canoe. Everything was ready. Glen slowly raised the pole, sunk its forked end in the water until it reached bottom, and shoved. As the boat crept through the water, he felt proud. He was now a wild ricer.

The two ricers worked carefully through a portion of the rice bed, then turned and headed back, just a few feet from their original path. Glen's father gave Glen time to get used to steering the sleek fiberglass canoe. He remembered the day nearly 30 years ago that he had first learned to harvest rice.

After making a couple of sweeping passes, the canoe came to a halt. Glen Sr. picked up a handful of wild rice. He scraped the husk from the rice and explained how you could tell by the color of the grain if the rice was ready to pick. When the grain was dark brown, it was ripe. He gestured toward the small pile of rice in the canoe. They were getting good rice, he said, because the long tails of the husks were standing up like the quills of a porcupine when it's scared.

Wild rice grows all the way across some parts of the Bowstring River. In other places, where the rice isn't so thick, the water is a deep blue.

Glen's father pointed to various places along the river. Upstream was Sand Lake, the river's source. Downstream, the river widened into Bowstring Lake. Glen Sr. explained that most of the rivers and lakes on the reservation were connected. He described how their ancestors had used these waterways to enter the area and take control of it from the Dakota Indians centuries earlier.

Glen's father said they should gather only as much rice as they needed for the coming year. Ducks and other birds also ate the rice, and what was left would fall back into the river so that the rice would grow again next year. Earlier in the summer, Glen's father had come out to the river alone. Glen knew he had sprinkled tobacco on the river as an offering for a good and safe harvest. Judging from the sprawling rice bed, the Creator had answered his father's prayers.

They headed for the landing. There was no sense in overdoing it on Glen's first day. He would need his rest, because tomorrow promised to be a long day. Not only would they go out on the river again, but they would also process the wild rice at his grandmother's house.

Glen and his father head back to the shore, where Glen's dog is waiting.

15

Wild rice, which the Ojibway call mahnomin, has long been an important food for Native Americans in the Upper Great Lakes region. Archaeologists, people who study past cultures, say that Indians gathered wild rice as far back as 2,500 years ago.

For the Ojibway people, wild rice is not only a basic food crop, but also has spiritual meaning. Stories handed down from generation to generation tell about a time when the Ojibway lived on the East Coast of North America. Prophets spoke of a great journey the Ojibway would have to make if they were to survive. The journey would be complete, the prophets said, only when the people reached a land where food grew abundantly in the water. This place would be their home, and the food a gift of the Creator.

The Ojibway migration took many hundreds of years. Finally, in the mid-1500s, the Ojibway found their special place, in what is now northern Minnesota and Wisconsin. Wild rice became a staple of their diet, helping them to survive the cold, harsh winters.

In the more than 400 years since the Ojibway arrived in the region, they have grown to be one of the largest nations of Indian people in North America. Ojibway reservations—land that the Ojibway kept through treaties with the U.S. government—are located throughout northern Minnesota and Wisconsin and in North Dakota and Michigan. Ojibway people also live in parts of Canada. More than 50,000 people are members of the 7 Ojibway reservations in Minnesota. Ojibway people are also referred to as Chippewa or Anishinaabeg.

Above: *Two ricing partners set out across a lake.* **Right:** *The grains of rice are ripe and ready to be harvested.*

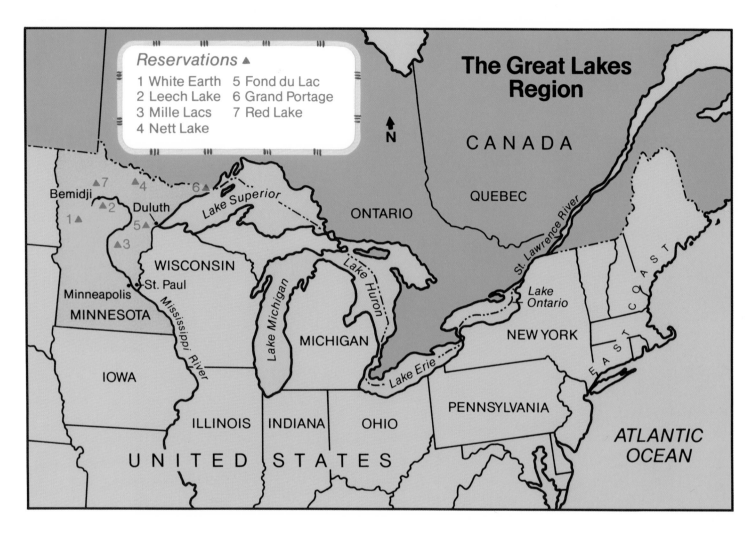

The map shows "The Great Lakes Region" with labels including CANADA, QUEBEC, ONTARIO, Lake Superior, Lake Huron, Lake Michigan, Lake Ontario, Lake Erie, St. Lawrence River, MICHIGAN, WISCONSIN, MINNESOTA, IOWA, ILLINOIS, INDIANA, OHIO, PENNSYLVANIA, NEW YORK, UNITED STATES, ATLANTIC OCEAN, EAST COAST, Mississippi River, Minneapolis, St. Paul, Duluth, Bemidji.

Reservations ▲

1 White Earth 5 Fond du Lac
2 Leech Lake   6 Grand Portage
3 Mille Lacs   7 Red Lake
4 Nett Lake

According to Ojibway history, the people migrated from the "Great Salt Sea" of the East Coast to the upper Great Lakes region. The map shows the seven Ojibway reservations in Minnesota.

The reservation where Glen lives is called Leech Lake. It has about 9,000 members. Almost half of them live on the reservation. Many others live in the Twin Cities of Minneapolis and St. Paul. Leech Lake is in north central Minnesota, in the heart of wild rice country. With 55 major wild rice beds on its lakes and rivers, the Leech Lake Reservation is one of the world's leading producers of natural wild rice.

*T*he next day was a good one for ricing. It had been a cool summer's night, the kind the elders in Glen's town say is needed for the wild rice to ripen. After only an hour out on the rice bed, Glen saw that the elders were right. He and his father had already filled the bottom of the canoe and they still had two more hours to harvest.

It was not even 10:00 and already the morning sun was heating up the still air. Glen could hear other harvesters on the river, but the tall rice stalks hid them from his view. Occasionally, in the distance, he spotted the tops of poles rising out of the rice bed.

Glen and his father began to develop a rhythm as rice was added to the pile. Every time the canoe slowed, Glen would quickly lift the pole from the water, slip it back in, and push off, keeping the boat moving at an easy pace. As the boat slid forward, his father reached over and used one knocker to bend the stalks of rice over the side of the canoe. With his free hand, he raised the other knocker and aimed for the tops of the stalks. *Swish!* The knockers found their mark and sent the rice grains flying into the canoe.

As the morning passes, the bottom of the canoe fills up with wild rice.

While yesterday had been meant for learning, this day was meant for working. Glen's muscles ached and he had blisters on his hands from poling the boat through the heavy stands of wild rice. Sweat glistened on his face. Glen was glad when his father told him to bring the canoe to a stop. As Glen lowered the pole and sat down, his father began to clean the rice, removing the dry, loose leaves and stems that had found their way into the boat.

Glen's uncle Steve and his ricing partner, Tony Jenkins, canoed over to where they were resting. The men talked about past ricing seasons and shared stories about their first harvests. Glen's father told them how easily Glen had learned to steer the canoe. Glen hoped he would become his father's steady ricing partner. Many ricers chose the same partner year after year, and steady ricing partners always seemed to be good friends.

Just before they were ready to start again, Glen's dog, Duke, swam up to the side of the canoe and tried to climb in. Glen steadied the boat so Duke wouldn't tip it over. He shooed Duke away, telling the dog it wasn't time for a swim. The four ricers had a good laugh.

Glen and his father meet Uncle Steve on the rice bed.

Soon the break was over and it was Glen's turn to become the knocker. It took some time for him to find his rhythm. Sometimes he barely got the rice to lean over the canoe before it would slip from his grasp. Other times, Glen would let fly with a mighty swing but miss the rice altogether. When that happened, his knocker would crash into the canoe, and a loud bang would echo across the river. Finally, after many tries, Glen began to bring in the rice!

The sun, now high in the sky, signaled the end of the day's harvest. Glen and his father made their way toward the landing, anxious to bag the day's pick. Onshore, they unloaded their gear and cleaned the rice. Glen Sr. said they had done well. They had harvested more than 100 pounds (45 kilograms) of wild rice. They packed the rice into narrow sacks, careful not to spill any of the sacred food. At last they were ready to make the trip to Grandmother's house to process the rice.

Glen and his father haul in their morning's harvest. Onshore, they stuff the scratchy wild rice into long sacks.

24

At a landing farther down the river, other Ojibway harvesters were docking their canoes loaded with rice. For these men and women, ricing is an annual activity. It is a time to visit with old friends and make new ones. It is a time for the harvesters to renew their connection to the river and to their heritage.

Many harvesters come from families who have riced in the area for generations. Like Glen, many are lifelong residents of Inger. Some of them come from other parts of the Leech Lake Reservation, and some make the four-hour car trip from Minneapolis.

Other harvesters bag their wild rice. Anyone who lives on the reservation, including non-Indians, can buy a ricing permit.

The government of the Leech Lake Reservation sets rules for the wild rice harvest. Government officers determine when the rice beds will be open, how many hours a day people can harvest—usually from 9:00 A.M. until noon—and who is allowed to harvest. The government sells a special permit to harvesters.

Only people who live on the reservation or are members of Leech Lake or another Ojibway reservation in Minnesota can buy permits. In some years, more than 2,000 people buy licenses to harvest wild rice on Leech Lake. This year, only 1,000 people bought the $2.00 permit. Those who did were blessed with a good harvest.

Many of the canoes coming in from the Bowstring River were nearly full. The better harvesters had brought in more than 300 pounds (135 kg). As people sacked their rice, the landing was filled with pleasant chatter. All of the ricers were satisfied with their day's pick.

Nearby, a rice buyer for the Leech Lake Reservation weighed the rice for harvesters who wanted to sell their rice. The reservation government, as well as independent rice buyers, purchase wild rice, then finish and package it to sell throughout the world. Some harvesters choose to sell their rice, while others, like Glen and his father, keep it for their own use.

In Inger, many people are busy weighing, buying, and selling wild rice.

Grandmother Susan's house is at the end of a dirt road a couple of miles outside of Inger. The house is surrounded by a forest of maple and birch trees.

When Glen and his parents arrived there, they had many things to do. It took a lot of work to finish the rice so that it would be ready to eat, but Glen knew it would be worth it. Besides, he would get to spend the rest of the day playing with his cousins.

Opposite: *Glen enjoys playing Nintendo with his cousins.*
Right: *Grandmother Susan.*
Below: *Family members spread the rice out on tarps to dry.*

The family members dumped the rice onto a plastic tarp to dry. Glen's father brought out a large cast-iron kettle and set it at an angle against two long, iron poles. The kettle would be used to parch the rice. Parching loosens the rice grains from the husks by cooking out the moisture. Eventually, the 100 pounds (45 kg) of rice that Glen and his father had brought in would be reduced to 50 pounds (23 kg) of finished wild rice.

While his father searched the area for firewood, Glen gathered twigs and sticks for kindling. They soon found enough wood and built a small fire underneath the kettle. When the kettle was hot, they carried the rice in traditional Ojibway birchbark containers to the cooking area.

Some of the rice was then put in the kettle, and Glen and his parents took turns stirring it. Grandmother Susan, who had parched rice for many years, told Glen that the constant stirring kept the rice from burning and helped it to cook evenly. When the batch was cooked just right—when the husks turned golden brown and started to separate from the grains—they poured it onto a tarp to cool. The process was repeated until all the rice was parched.

Glen Sr. uses birch wood to start a fire for the parching. Parching cooks the moisture out of the wild rice.

Glen takes his turn at parching.

Glen's family has always parched rice in this way. Some Ojibway people parch rice in large metal containers that can hold much more rice than a kettle. These metal containers are heated by wood fires, and paddles inside the containers turn the rice to prevent it from burning. Commercial wild rice producers—companies that sell wild rice to the public—parch rice in huge metal cylinders over gas flames. Grandma Susan told Glen that their family's method was slower, but the rice became softer and the finished rice didn't take as long to cook. Besides, she said, it tasted better than rice finished by other methods.

Commercial wild rice producers finish large quantities of rice at a time. Inset: The commercial wild rice is parched in large metal cylinders.

The next step was the jigging, which would grind the husk away from the rice kernel. Jigging is done by "dancing" on the rice. Glen's father changed from his hard-soled shoes into soft leather moccasins so the rice grains wouldn't break too easily. Glen and his father found a small wooden bucket, filled it about one-quarter full of parched rice, and began to dance on it.

Grandma Susan pours the parched rice into a birch-bark basket.

34

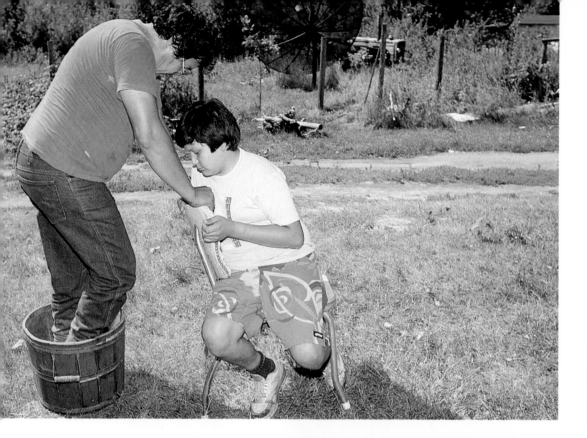

Glen watches as his father does the jigging "dance." Below: *The family takes a break to give their dog a little attention.*

Every so often Glen's father would stop, grab a handful of the rice, and examine it. When he could no longer see any husks attached to the grains, he took the rice out of the bucket and added more. This part of the process was slow and tiresome. Finally, after what seemed like hours to Glen, the jigging was complete.

The family then began the last step before the rice was ready to be cooked and eaten. They dumped the rice from the bucket back into the birchbark containers. The ground-up husks—now called chaff—had to be separated, or "winnowed," from the rice. This is done by lightly tossing the rice in the air so that the wind blows the chaff away and the heavier rice grains fall back into the container.

Glen's father teaches him how to winnow the wild rice before Glen gets his chance to try it.

Glen's father and grand-mother showed him their winnowing technique before letting him do it. On his first try, Glen lost nearly half the rice from the basket. After a few more tries, he got the hang of it and was soon able to winnow without super-vision. Finally, enough of the rice was finished to make a meal. When Grandmother headed for the house with the finished rice, Glen knew that he would soon be enjoy-ing a taste of his first wild rice harvest.

Wild rice has been called the perfect food. It is high in protein, carbohydrates, and fiber, but low in fat. Actually, wild rice is not a true rice like white rice, but a grain that grows on top of a long grass. It grows best under certain conditions. The rivers and lakes where it grows must have muddy bottoms, and the soil must be stirred so that the wild rice seeds get the oxygen and nutrients they need to sprout. This stirring happens when the snow and ice melt in the spring, causing flooding.

In late April, when the water in the lake or river warms up, the seeds sprout and anchor their roots into the newly stirred soil. Then the plant begins to grow, drawing its food from the rich soil and its energy from the sun. Finally, during the warm days and cool nights of late August and early September, the plant ripens and its grains are ready to be gathered.

The Upper Great Lakes region is one of the few places in the world with ideal conditions for wild rice to grow naturally. In a good harvest year, only a few million pounds of natural, finished wild rice are produced worldwide. In contrast, the yearly harvest of white rice is about 520 short tons (470 million metric tons)—that's about 200 pounds (90 kg) for each person on earth. The scarcity of wild rice has helped to make it valuable, because people are willing to spend more money for a product that's hard to find. But this scarcity has also led to the domestication of wild rice.

In the late 1960s, scientists at the University of Minnesota developed a type of wild rice that does not break easily when it is harvested by machines. This new strain made it possible for wild rice to grow in large flooded fields called paddies. Paddy rice can be harvested by combine machines similar to those used by farmers to harvest wheat and corn. More than 30 million pounds (14 million kg) of wild rice are produced on paddies in California, Minnesota, and Canada.

The increase in the yearly wild rice harvest has caused its price to drop. In the early 1970s, wild rice sold for as much as $20 a pound in some parts of the world. Now it can be bought for as little as $2 a pound.

While paddy rice may be good for the consumer, it has hurt the Ojibway harvesters. Twenty years ago, a wild ricer could earn more than $3,000 during a good season. Now $1,000 is considered a good year.

The finished product, packaged and ready to be sold—Leech Lake wild rice

Uncle Steve gives Glen his first bite of the wild rice he harvested. It's a proud moment for Glen. Meanwhile, a friend eagerly waits for a taste.

Grandma Susan came from her house carrying a pot of cooked wild rice. She spread a blanket on the ground and asked Glen to sit down. Glen's father, his uncle Steve, and some of his cousins joined him.

Before they ate the rice, Grandmother talked about the importance of Glen's first wild rice harvest. It was a way for Glen to learn about his people's history, she said, and to know that rice meant survival to the Ojibway. By harvesting rice, Glen could feel that he was a part of the natural world. She then asked the Creator to bless her grandson. Glen ate a spoonful of the wild rice. He loved its soft texture and sweet, nutty taste. It was delicious!

Later that evening, Glen felt sad that he had only one more day left to harvest rice before returning to school for the new term. Tomorrow Glen's father would return to his job as a truck driver for the state highway department, and the two wouldn't be able to rice together again this season. But Glen would go with his mother for one last day on the rice bed.

At school, Glen tells his friends about his first harvest.

Wild rice will make many delicious dinners for Glen and his parents during the coming year.

Already, Glen was looking forward to next year's harvest. He knew that when the cool nights of late summer arrived, he and his parents would look to the lakes and the rivers. They would once again prepare their canoes in anticipation of the sacred harvest.

Word List

chaff—the husks of the rice after they are separated from the grains

Dakota—American Indian people from the Great Plains; also called Sioux

domestication—the scientific adaptation of natural wild rice so that it could be grown in paddies

elder—an older person who is respected and admired for his or her knowledge and experience

finish—to prepare the harvested rice so that it is ready to be cooked and eaten

husk—the outer covering of the rice grain

jigging—the part of the finishing process when the rice is placed in a bucket and stepped or "danced" on so that the husks come off the grains

knockers—long, slender wooden sticks that are used to knock the grains of wild rice from the plant

license—a permit allowing its holder to do or buy something

mahnomin—wild rice; considered a sacred food by the Ojibway Indians

Ojibway—American Indian people from the Great Lakes area; also called Anishinaabeg or Chippewa

paddy—a flooded field suitable for growing rice

parch—to heat the wild rice so that the moisture is cooked out of it

prophet—a person with special wisdom

reservation—areas of land that Indian people kept through treaties with the U.S. government

tobacco—in many Native American cultures, tobacco is burned or sprinkled as an offering to the Creator

winnow—the part of the finishing process when the rice is fanned or tossed into the air and the husks separate from the grains

For Further Reading

Broker, Ignatia. *Night Flying Woman.* St. Paul: Minnesota Historical Society Press, 1983.

Johnston, Basil H. *Tales the Elders Told: Ojibway Legends.* Ontario: Royal Ontario Museum, 1981.

Osinski, Alice K. *The Chippewa.* Chicago: Childrens Press, 1987.

Peyton, John L. *The Stone Canoe and Other Stories.* Blacksburg, Virginia: The McDonald & Woodward Pub. Co., 1989.

Snake, Sam, et al. *The Adventures of Nanabush: Ojibway Indian Stories.* New York: Atheneum, 1980.

Tanner, Helen Hornbeck. Frank W. Porter III, gen. ed. *The Ojibwa.* New York: Chelsea House Pub., 1992.

About the Contributors

Author **Gordon Regguinti** is a member of the Leech Lake Band of Ojibway. He was raised on Leech Lake Reservation by his mother and grandparents. As he grew up, he learned to value the changing of the seasons as he helped grow vegetables, pick berries, and collect sap from maple trees to make maple sugar and syrup. As a young man, Regguinti began to harvest wild rice on Leech Lake. Regguinti's Ojibway heritage has remained a central focus of his professional life. A graduate of the University of Minnesota with a B.A. in Indian Studies, he has written about Native American issues for newspapers and school curricula. He served as editor of the American Indian newspaper *The Circle* for two years and was the coordinator of the Two Rivers Native Film and Video Festival in 1991. Regguinti is managing editor of *Colors*, a magazine for people of color. He lives in Minneapolis and has six children and one grandchild.

Photographer **Dale Kakkak** was born and raised in the Menominee Nation. He is the staff photographer for *The Circle*, a native newspaper in the Twin Cities. He is a poet, fiction writer, and student of life.

Series Consultant **W. Roger Buffalohead**, Ponca, has been involved in Indian Education for more than 20 years, serving as a national consultant on issues of Indian curricula and tribal development. He has a B.A. in American History from Oklahoma State University and an M.A. from the University of Wisconsin, Madison. Buffalohead has taught at the University of Cincinnati, the University of California, Los Angeles, and the University of Minnesota, where he was director of the American Indian Learning and Resources Center from 1986 to 1991. Currently he teaches at the American Indian Arts Institute in Santa Fe, New Mexico. Among his many activities, Buffalohead is a founding board member of the National Indian Education Association and a member of the Cultural Concerns Committee of the National Conference of American Indians. He lives in Santa Fe.

Series Consultant **Juanita G. Corbine Espinosa**, Dakota/Ojibway, serves as director of Native Arts Circle, Minnesota's first statewide Native American arts agency. She is first and foremost a community organizer, active in a broad range of issues, many of which are related to the importance of art in community life. In addition, she is a board member of the Minneapolis American Indian Center and an advisory member of the Minnesota State Arts Board's Cultural Pluralism Task Force. She was one of the first people to receive the state's McKnight Human Service Award. She lives in Minneapolis.